HOW BLOG GOT 1 MILLION VISITS IN 7 MONTHS

A practical and straightforward guide to increasing traffic to your blog in your spare time - and without having to pay for advertising.

PATRIC MORGAN

Overview
All Web Site Data

AUDIENCE

Visits

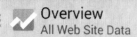 1,004,463

1 915,443 from United Kingdom

2 21,628 from United States

3 13,664 from Australia

4 5,747 from Canada

5 4,777 from Germany

6 3,617 from Spain

7 3,517 from Ireland

8 3,090 from France

9 3,033 from New Zealand

10 2,598 from Netherlands

+192 other countries / territories

"Patric Morgan's How My Blog Got 1 Million Visitors in 7 Months makes me sick! I've got 15,000+ people on my combined social media and I've never gotten even close to a million visits on my site. Screw you, Patric! However – I have read through his book and have found some cool tricks to steal and apply. Shh...don't tell him."
Vicki Abelson, Author of 'Don't Jump', published October '15 from Carl Reiner's Random Content.

"What an absolutely incredible 'How to Guide'. This book will give you the tools you need to increase your web traffic and create a viral sensation from your blog or website. Follow the common sense approach within these pages and maybe you'll be writing your own success story very soon. A must read for any avid blogger trying to step up into the big leagues. Buy it now!"
Nigel Shinner, Author of the critically acclaimed novel 'From Within'

"It's good to read something that actually delivers on the title of the book. You've inspired me to really believe in my blog and you've given me the knowledge to fill in the gaps that I was struggling with."
Kath Formosa-Bown, Features Writer and Marketing Consultant, 'Mail On Sunday Book of the Week'

Contents

Part Five

Part Six

Part Seven

About The Author

FOREWORD

Blogging has never been bigger. For some, blogging is a pastime, a hobby, something to fulfil a creative need. But some take blogging one step further.

Many individuals, with no special training, are using their blog/s as a part-time or even a full-time job. You may already have a blog that could do with a few more visitors. Or maybe you're thinking of setting up a blog but are not sure where to start.

The question most people ask me is 'How do I get visitors to my blog?' It's like setting up a shop on the High Street and facing the challenge of getting people in the door.

The good news is – I have answers that will see your visitor count lift substantially. All you need is a computer, an internet connection and a brain (your own preferably).

Here's what you don't need: money.

This book answers your blogging questions in a practical and straightforward way. *How My Blog Got 1 Million Visits In 7 Months* has been designed to show you how to drive people to your blog – and how to keep them coming back, time after time. It's designed for bloggers and for those who have websites that could do with more traffic.

I'm a multi-award winning blogger and publisher and have been for over eight years. When I first started blogging, I got very excited to see that one person kept visiting my site. That was until I realised that the analytics was, in fact, counting me as a visitor. I've learned a lot since. My latest blog broke through the 1,000,000 visit mark after just 7 months. As a result, my blog is now a profitable business. I haven't spent a penny on advertising and I spend about 30 minutes a day blogging at most. I've picked up a large-scale book deal as a direct result of my blog.

In this book, I'll show you the basics of setting up your blog; how to write content that people will just want to click on and share with their friends; how to create viral posts that will see your visitor statistics balloon; how to write content for your website that will sell your services or products; how to optimise your posts for search engines and how to make money from your blog.

My promise to you is this - if you use the tips and tricks that I am about to show you, your site will get more traffic and you can start making money from it. These are proven techniques that you can start implementing on your blog straight away.

Run the kind of blog that other bloggers envy.

Be the kind of blogger that people marvel at. It'll make you feel pretty good, I guarantee it.

Find out how right now.

INTRO

On 14th March 2015, I went to watch my team Wales play Ireland at Cardiff's Millennium Stadium. I love my rugby and my friend Ian and I were chuffed to bits to have seats right on the halfway line for the Six Nations showdown.

A few days earlier, I had published a blog post on my spoof news website WalesOnCraic that had gone viral. The post carried a story that members of staff at the Millennium Stadium were able to tilt the pitch each side of half time so that the Irish players were playing uphill for the entire game. It seemed the only way that Wales could beat Ireland – that's how tough a prospect Ireland had been ahead of the game!

In just a few short days, the post received over 80,000 individual visitors. Through techniques I'll be showing you shortly, the post generated more than enough income to pay for our tickets and our beer for the entire day!

I distinctly remember looking around in marvel at this great Welsh stadium, with its cacophony of 74,500 spectators baying on the gladiators in red for a Welsh win. And I remember thinking 'More than all these people together took the time to click on my blog post'. It was quite a humbling moment but one that made me realise the potential of blogging, both as a creative outlet, and as a way of earning extra income.

I've written this book to show you how you too can get huge amounts of traffic to your blog at no or very little cost.

So why am I sharing this information with you?

Well, to be honest, I keep getting asked the same question by bloggers – 'how do you do it?' Well it's all here – everything I do. I like to think of myself as a kind person and anyway, it's always nice to share. For my part, this should allow me to get on with my day job as a magazine publisher instead of being constantly questioned. I've got a fair amount of blogging knowledge that I've built up over the years, all of it self-taught. It's something you can do too – there's no need to have any special set of skills but obviously, the more talented you are as a writer, the better chance of success with your blog.

With this book, you too could have an acclaimed blog that people love – and a blog that can earn you a decent amount of income that can pay off a few of those bills or pay for a good few holidays. If you are serious about blogging, I guarantee that this book will put a smile on your face.

What could possibly be better than getting paid over and over again for just 30 minutes of work a day? This is how we're going to do this: I'm going to explain my background and credentials and give you the brief story of the blog that got me 1 million visits. Then I'll show you where to start your blogging journey (if you haven't started it already). After that, I'll give you all the gubbins on how to create viral content, and maximise it on social media. Then finally, I'll show you how you can make money from your blog. This isn't a get rich quick book either so don't go giving up your day job just yet!

PART ONE

What This Book Is

This book is a practical guide to being successful at blogging, either as an amateur or as a professional. I've deliberately avoided making this a step-by-step guide, namely because the processes often change. Instead, I'm laying out the concepts and ideas that can increase traffic to your blog. As a result, you'll be glad to know that this isn't the longest book in the world. I'm hoping that you can just take some of my ideas and get busy blogging!

Your blog could well go on to be better than mine – I genuinely hope it does. Let me know if you do well and I'll feature your story in future editions of this book! You'll find my email address in the back pages.

My Background and Credentials

This part isn't an ego trip. That's not my style. Instead, this part is here so that I can show you that I'm a pretty normal guy, with a pretty normal background – just like most people. I wasn't born with a silver spoon in my mouth (most Welsh people aren't) and have received no formal training when it comes to blogging. I started work at 15, working in an office on a dockside; I've worked in kebab shops (horrid), clothes shops (nasty) and call centres (the place where souls go to die). I got myself a degree in Communication Studies but I've never really used it effectively to get myself the jobs I wanted.

When it comes to employment, I've not been particularly lucky either. In 2002, I got made redundant twice from sales jobs within three months. As I was fairly new in both jobs, I wasn't entitled to any payments of any kind. In fact, in the second redundancy, where I worked for a company called the Accident Group (yep – the 'Where there's blame, there's a claim' rubbish!), we were all laid off by text message. Charming.

In 2007, I moved to a suburb of Cardiff and with my business partner, set up a community magazine. We'd both racked up a huge amount of debt on our credit cards and needed to do something to clear them. We had no capital for our new magazine – we had to raise money for our first print run by getting adverts sold without even having a product to show anyone. That was a tough gig, and looking back, I'm not really sure how we got off the ground. From the way I felt a year later, I'm sure it came down to sheer hard work and tenacity.

One of the main concepts of the magazine was to ensure that it was a quality product. We didn't want to peddle one of those rag mags that were stuffed full of adverts. We worked hard at the editorial side of things to ensure that the magazines were actually read. That way, our lovely advertisers had more chance of having their adverts seen and acted on.

When we first launched, we paid a company to deliver our magazines to the local area but we found that the lazy chumps stopped delivering to people's houses when they got to hills (Wales is a hilly, mountainous place!). This was on our second issue which was even worse than having it not delivered on the first issue as people were expecting it! We had to finance the printing of our third issue ourselves so that our advertisers weren't left out of pocket.

The following year saw the recession bite. A few of the local businesses folded but thankfully, our magazines seemed unfazed by it. A few of our competitor magazines also folded, I think partly due to the fact that they didn't invest in the quality of their product. I'll come on to this later – there's a reason I'm telling you all this.

Despite the tough start, our magazines are still as popular as ever and have gone on to win some prestigious national awards - in 2014, we picked up two gongs at the UK Independent Magazine Awards – one for Best Editorial and the other for Best Website.

In 2007, I became an English teacher, a profession I enjoyed for several years. I walked away in 2010, frustrated that all the Headmasters were hiring Teaching Assistants to do the job I was qualified to do. The same year, I started work for a company called A4E. In training, we were made to watch a video about its big boss lady, who lived in some mansion somewhere in England. The video explained to us how clever she was and what an inspiration she was (she wasn't – not to me at any rate). Then, two months later, they sacked me for 'not hitting targets'. I'd never been sacked before in my life and even as the words were coming out of my manager's mouth, I knew that I would never go back to working for other people. In my view, most of them were insincere and not the kind of people you wanted to hang out with anyway. The following day, I took delivery of our latest issue of the magazines and spent 14 hours walking non-stop to deliver them. I came home, having got all my anger out, and flopped into bed.

Ever since, I've worked for myself. I've gleaned all my newfound confidence from things I've managed to achieve myself. I've never had a manager telling me how crap I was, or how they wanted things done for years. I've been thanked by total strangers for my work and I've also gone on to win other awards. In 2012, I picked up 'Best Writing on a Blog' at the Wales Blog Awards. Strangely enough, my sister won the same award the very next year. Apart from a few bits and bobs I learned during my degree, I've never had any formal training for the things I do now.

I'm mostly self-taught (which I'll also come onto a little later). I've always enjoyed writing and blogging seemed a natural progression for people to read my work. My point is this - you don't need any specific skillsets to become a good blogger. As you progress up the blogging ladder, you will increase your knowledgebase and become more of an expert in both your field, and at blogging.

I'm not sure where you are right now on your blogging journey. You may already run a popular and well-loved blog. On the other hand, you may be considering creating one.

Either way, by reading this book and implementing the strategies and know-how that I'm about to show you, you will have more blogging ability than a lot of bloggers out there right now.

Before I tell you how to do it, I need to briefly tell you about the blog that got me over 1 million visits in less than 7 months. I'm hoping that it will inspire you.

The WalesOnCraic Story

This book revolves around my blog called WalesOnCraic which I set up at the end of August 2014. It has never been the best blog in the world but its roots do go back a long way. I need to explain its background because, as I will explain later, it forms the basis for a good blog.

As a kid growing up in Barry, South Wales, I loved nothing more than heading down to my local corner shop and buying myself a new exercise book. I'd rip out a good wedge of the pages and then staple them together again to create a 'magazine' that I'd write in felt-tip pen. I called it *Zut* because that was the only word I learned in French lessons. I only ever made two copies of each magazine – one for my immediate family and one for my cousins who lived in Cardiff. I'd send their copy by post and my favourite issues were the autumn and winter ones because I loved being cosy. My younger brother, who also loved being cosy, set up one of his own magazines and called it *The Cosy Mag*. Every issue, he'd feature a 'Cosy Item Of The Month' – it could have been a pair of slippers or a cup of tea. Ultimately, he only ever did issues for October, November and December because there was no call for 'cosy' things during the other warmer months of the year.

When I think back, the ultimate aim of my magazines was to entertain people. I've still got them somewhere and they are a very childish attempt at humour. Around that time, I had a ZX Spectrum 48k computer – the one with the hard plastic keys, not the traditional rubber keys. As a result, I also used to pick up a magazine called *Your Sinclair*. It had a huge impact on me. *Your Sinclair* was like nothing I'd ever read before (or since). Thinking about heading down to the local WH Smiths store to pick up my latest issue was something that kept me going through my boring school lessons.

What set *Your Sinclair* apart was its comedic, informal narrative style. Its beauty was that it provided readers with the information they were seeking but in a totally different way. The magazine had many 'characters' writing for them (I've only recently

14

discovered that the magazine was only written by a handful of people who wrote under various pen names). Each character had a certain style of writing and had their own (fictional) back-story. The magazine also contained non-computer stuff - things like the Peculiar Pets Corner that was originally intended to be a showcase for *YS* readers' exotic pets such as snakes, pigs, monkeys or spiders. It ended up including such things as a purple fruit gum and a tuba.

Looking back now, it's easy to define who their target audience was – teenagers like me, who had a ZX Spectrum, enjoyed playing games, but didn't take it all too seriously. There were other magazines for the real geeks and my God, they were dull. *Your Sinclair* was for me, a breath of fresh air, and a huge inspiration. Head to www.ysrnry.co.uk to see what I mean.

The most important thing for me was that the magazine made me **feel** as if I was one of them – part of an exclusive club. They talked about things that I was familiar with and reached out to me in a way that made me feel that I was part of a shared experience. I'll talk about that more in depth later. It's the key to creating viral blog posts.

WalesOnCraic came about at the end of a three hour breakfast at a Wetherspoons pub in Merthyr. I'd met up with my friends Bunko and Lyn to discuss the possibility of setting up a website. Its aim would be to showcase Welsh comedy. Bunko had got in touch as I was running a comedy blog for Wales called Derek the Weathersheep which was proving popular on Facebook. If you don't live in Wales or even know where it is, I'll need to explain a few things:

- Firstly, Wales is not in England. It's not part of England. It's separate. But we are part of the UK. We're in it with England, Scotland and Northern Ireland.

-       In Wales, we have a very lovely weatherman on our TV called Derek who is a well-loved celebrity. We also have a lot of sheep.

It sounds a bit bizarre but the idea of Derek the Weathersheep came to me as I was sat waiting in my car at a zebra crossing. This kid with fluffy white hair was on his way to school with his mum and he looked up at a big black cloud that was lurking overhead as he crossed the crossing. I set up the blog and called it Derek the Weathersheep, the idea being that 'Derek' would post daily weather forecasts for Wales. Unexpectedly, the blog took off and became very popular, picking up a big following on Facebook over the course of a year or so. The blog would ultimately be a forerunner of WalesOnCraic – the blog that got me over a million visits in seven months. Derek the Weathersheep was important as it formed my training ground for posting viral content. It's where I learned the techniques that I'm about to share with you (yes, I'll get on to it asap – I just need to give you some background and context).

The first posts on WalesOnCraic were rehashes of things that both Bunko and I had written before. I shared them on Facebook accounts that I'd already had, one of them being Derek the Weathersheep because of its similar target audience. The original plan was to spoof news items that appeared in the real news but as the weeks went on, we found our material was more original than we had intended. Bunko also posted less and less as he'd been asked to write two books for a local publisher.

But within a few weeks, WalesOnCraic was pulling in visitor figures that I could have only dreamt of. It became a bit of a monster.

Ok. So I've bored you to death with some background information and you want to get onto the nitty-gritty.

In Part Two, I'll explain how I did it. If you follow the processes I did, you will see your visitor figures rise too.

Are you ready?

Ok. Let's begin.

PART TWO

Where To Start

Before you start unleashing your blog on the world, you need to be totally honest with yourself and ask yourself the following questions. The reason you need to mull these over is because if you're anything like me, you'll start a blog and get bored after a few weeks.

Here are the questions:

-        Is your blog going to be (or is it already) something that is part of you? What I mean by that is, will this come naturally, or will you have to work at it? Chances are, that if you have to work at it, you will struggle to maintain it. I've found that on a few of my blogs, I've had a flash of inspiration, set up a blog, and a month later, found it languishing without any regular updates.

-        Are you ready for some people to not like what you've written? The bigger your following, the more chance that you're going to find someone who doesn't like your work. That's fine. It's fine because the more you divide your audience, the more you can find your niche – the ones who like your work and the ones who will become lifelong fans and keep coming back for more. I'll talk about finding your niche in the next section. It's possibly THE most important bit!

-        Are you able to commit? My Derek the Weathersheep blog required daily posts. When I set it up, I imagined myself getting up every morning, brewing up a lovely coffee and merrily posting a weather update. Sadly, there were mornings when I was a) too busy b) too tired c) too hungover or d) out of the country, to commit to sitting down and penning another witty weather forecast. I'd end up making excuses that Derek was hungover (which were based on truth). People seemed to find the idea of a hungover sheep endearing and they soon forgave him but that wasn't the intention. But seriously consider how much time you can devote to your blog. I spend on average 30 minutes a day on WalesOnCraic but you may want to post less frequently than I do. Whatever you do, try and keep it consistent – don't post like a fiend for three days and then take three months off. What will happen is that you will return and start a new post with the dreaded 'Sorry I haven't posted for a while…' cliché.

- Are you in this for the fame, money, or just for the love of it? Chances are that if you are in it for fame and fortune, you won't make it. Personally, I like to read blogs that show people's passion for what they do or love, not for fame. If you're passionate about things, good things will follow naturally.

- Remember that your story is unique. You have a story to tell that no one else has. Are you going to keep it quiet? Who else is going to tell it? Don't be ashamed or embarrassed like I was when I first set out.

If you haven't got a blog set up yet, you may have a good idea of what you want to write about. But before you start typing, you need to work backwards. If you are writing a blog to keep to yourself, that's fine. But if you are creating a blog that you'd like to succeed, you need to think about who you are writing for.

This is critical to the success of your blog.

I used to teach GCSE English and I was always banging on about 'the audience'. This is the place to start, not what the blog looks like or what you are going to write. Everything else that you do will fall into place if you know who you are writing for. Ask any top writer and they will tell you specifically, the type of people they are writing for, both in general, and specifically, with each publication.

Put simply – if you don't know who you are writing for, your blog will suck.

Fortunately, I'll show you how you can find yours.

Finding Your Niche and Target Audience

This is probably the most important chapter in the book. It is the key to your blogging success – the foundations if you like. Build a house on sand and before long, it'll soon start to present you with all sorts of problems.

My wife won't mind me telling you this, but for her, our wedding day sucked. After all the stress of preparing, she couldn't relax at all. Why? Well, she was trying to keep everyone happy for the entire day. Eventually, exhausted, she flopped into a chair around a table of her closest friends. For the next hour or two, she did nothing apart from devote her time to the ones who knew her best. And that's where she (and her friends) got the most out of the day. Of course, some of the people who weren't sat around the table moaned that the coffee didn't arrive on time, or that the music was too loud. But hey – they had gobbled down a free lunch so who were they to moan?

My point is this: don't try and keep everyone happy. It will never work.

That's rule No1. What you are after is a NICHE.

I'll say that again because it is so important -

What you are after is a NICHE.

Let's have a little experiment. Get a pen and paper. Go on. I'll wait.

Now. Let's pretend that you're considering setting up a blog that covers motor sports. I want you to write down everything that you can think of that's related to motor sports. Everything and anything. Set yourself a limit of five minutes and then come back to me.

Done it?

Good.

I guarantee you that whatever you've written down covers less than 5% of ALL motor sports, probably less than that. I'm a huge fan of drag racing – which is classed as a motor sport (0-100mph in less than one second; 0-300mph in just 3-4 seconds – what's not to like?) Yet, when I sit down to find some drag racing on TV, I'll click into Motor Sports and find myself faced with F1, F2, F3, tractor racing, motocross, speed boating, banger racing – the list goes on and on. Do you think I can find drag racing? No. You see my point? If you set up a blog about motor sports, those who want to find your blog via Google will have no idea where to start. How is your target audience supposed to find you?

So, if you were setting up a blog for motor sport, you're going to need to think a bit cleverer than that. What's your angle? Is it for people trying to get into motorsport? Is it a page celebrating the history of the British motor racing? Is it about the safety of motor sport? Whatever it is, the smaller the better – a microniche if you like. I'll write that in bold so you don't miss it.

Rule No2: The smaller your niche, the better. A microniche if you like.

Sounds stupid right? Wrong. I've set up blogs

that are so all-encompassing, that I have no idea where to start and walked away from it before I have even started.

WalesOnCraic's niche is the people of Wales. Narrow that down further and I guess you could nail it as a 'spoof Welsh news blog' – I don't know of any other 'spoof Welsh news blogs' although I'm sure one day, someone will set another one up. Ideally, I could narrow my niche down even further to Welsh cities – CardiffOnCraic, SwanseaOnCraic and so on – they would prove uber-successful. Sadly, I simply don't have the time as the success of WalesOnCraic has opened new doors for me.

You may find that you set up several blogs before you find the one that really works. By experimenting, you can then figure out what works and what doesn't work. Before WalesOnCraic, I had several attempts at something similar before I discovered what people loved sharing, especially on Weathersheep. It's where I honed my skills.

If someone criticises or dislikes your post, simply consider them as outside your target audience. These are the people who complained about the coffee arriving late at my wedding. I'm sure they've forgotten about it (I haven't!) but ultimately, they are important to you because you are learning what works and what doesn't. You can then focus on being good at the things that do work.

Planning

Like most things in life, if you don't plan, you're doomed to fail. Here's another boring story: in 1989, I sat my English GCSE exam. As part of the Imaginative Writing section, I had to write a short story. I remember reading somewhere shortly before I went in to my exam that I had to add a twist at the end. As an established writer now, I work backwards in my writing – planning the ending and adding the start last. But back then, I got stuck into the first title that I saw and got writing. I went at it like the clappers.

After ten minutes, I realised that I didn't know where the story was going. Worse still, I didn't know how to end it. I spent 20 minutes trying to figure out where the story could go and before I knew it, I had five minutes left to finish it. In the end, I finished the story abruptly by having my character walking out into the street and getting run over by a car. The ending came from nowhere and was totally out of character with the rest of the story. I can see the examiner in my mind's eye now – shaking their head and tutting.

As an English teacher, I always pressed home the importance of planning.

Here's what you need to consider with your blog:

-       Who are you writing for? Don't write things for yourself. Unless you have been to the moon or transplanted someone's head onto a giraffe, most people don't want to know about your visits to the local supermarket or what you had for tea last night. Make a connection with the reader in some way (more on this shortly).
-       What style are you going to adopt? This is important to get right at the start because people resist change. I originally set up my Derek the Weathersheep blog as a way of spreading a vegetarian message, believe it or not. I'd seen a TV show called *Kill It, Cook It, Eat It* a few days earlier and saw two little lambs wandering into the studio, unaware that the audience were about to watch them being killed. My aim was to build up readers' love for the characters and then show how

cruel it was to have their kids taken away at Easter when everyone traditionally eats lamb. Finally, when Easter came around, I posted a blog about the lambs going missing and hinted that the readers were the likely culprits as they were the ones settling down to eat poor old lambs. The post got one 'like' on Facebook – not really the earth-shattering moment I had envisaged. As it was, I had to maintain the style I'd created and not delve too much into 'serious' stuff. Lesson learnt!

-        How regularly are you going to post? I touched on this in the last section but it is worth building into your plan. Remember people only spend a matter of seconds (minutes if you're lucky) on your site. But everyone who does visit leaves that all-important 'Visit' figure to your stats.

Self-learning

As far as my blogging goes, I'm totally self-taught.

That's good news for you because it means that you don't need any particular special set of skills to get a good blog going. If you're lucky enough to be a talented writer, you're onto a winner!

I went to Uni, got my degree but I've never used it to get a job. I've spent the last seven years teaching myself how to blog and get it to my target audience. There are plenty of ways to self-teach. The internet is probably the best source of information. Practically every question you ask about blogging, you can find an answer online. YouTube offers many video tutorials, usually free, and I've learned a lot that way.

Don't think you can't run a successful blog because you don't have the knowledge. You CAN have the knowledge – you just need to Google it!

PART THREE

Setting Up Your Blog

I'm presuming here that you're new to blogging so I've included this chapter to give you a basic guide to setting up your blog. You will find plenty of other resources about setting a blog up online if you need additional detailed information. If you already have an established blog, you may want to scan this chapter to see if there's anything you've missed in setting up your site. It could mean the difference between getting ten visits and ten thousand!

When you're setting up your blog, the first thing you'll need to do is decide on your blog name. Make it specific to your niche if you can. I often see vans driving around my city with things like AJ Services written on the side. What the hell do they do? I saw one once with ElectroMend on the side. Alright, cheesy, but at least I had some idea of what they do! Fixing electrical stuff is my guess.

Once you've settled on a name, you'll now need to decide on which platform you want to run your blog from. This is software from which you will run your online operation. Don't worry too much if you decide to swap platforms at a later date – there are ways of transferring blogs to a new platform.

There are several platforms I've used in the past and they've all been free. Blogger is a great way to find your feet if you're new to blogging. You don't need to download anything as it's all run online. It's pretty straightforward and you can add your own styling to your blog. I won't go into too much detail on it here - head over to www.blogger.com and have a rummage around to see if it's for you. It's all perfectly self-explanatory.

Wordpress.com is halfway between Blogger and Wordpress (which I will explain in more detail shortly as this is the platform I use the most). Like Blogger, your site is stored on their servers so you don't need to worry about paying anyone! Have a look at www.wordpress.com to see if this suits what you plan to do with your blog.

My platform of choice is Wordpress. To work with this, you'll need to register your domain name (eg www.walesoncraic.com) with a host. I use one.com whose site is pretty easy to work with.

Go to www.one.com and search for a domain name that you like (hopefully it will match the name of your blog) and if it's available, buy it. It'll only cost about a tenner (GBP) and the reason I stay with them is that 'back in the day', when you had do everything technical yourself, they were on hand with their 24 hour chat helpline. They've helped me out of a few scrapes in the past. Your blog will be stored on a shared server (you can obviously log in from your computer) but if you find that you're getting millions of visitors within a few days, you may need to upgrade (possible but unlikely). If you are using One.com, you will be taken through the set-up process on screen.

Once you have access to your Control Panel (most of this you will never use as it's fairly technical), you can create your own email address (which will look pretty professional and can be accessed via a webmail page. You can also add your email account to your Outlook if you use it – Google the process if you don't know how to do it). Look for the 1-click Wordpress button on your dashboard and click on that. Again, this is miles simpler than it used to be and the onscreen guide will take you through the process.

Click 'Install' and Wordpress will automatically upload to your web address (or home page URL). You'll be given a log in page (this is usually your webpage with the suffix /wp-admin following it). You will be asked to set up a Username and Password and once these are saved, you can then use these on your /wp-admin page to log into your dashboard. It's useful to bookmark the admin page on your browsers (Explorer, Firefox, Chrome etc.) so you can get to it easily.

I've shortened the process a little here but again, you can find ways to install Wordpress out there on the internet, especially if you are using another host. Most hosts try to make it as easy as possible to upload Wordpress to your site. There is plenty of documentation on the installation process and I'm keen to show you the techniques I've used to get thousands of visitors to my blogs instead of going over it with a fine-toothed comb! I hope you understand.

There are a few settings I would recommend changing however:

First thing you need to do is scroll down to settings and change the following
-       Under Settings>General Settings, add a catchy tagline and hit 'Save'.
-       Under Settings>Permalinks, select Post Name and hit 'Save'. When you publish a post, this will generate a URL that contains the keywords from your heading. This is important for Search Engines, which I will come onto shortly.
-       Via Appearance>Themes, you can then browse their collection of themes. These are templates that create the look of your blog. You obviously know

your blog better than me so spend time browsing and figuring out which one would work best for you. Most of the ones you can see on Wordpress are free but if you're serious about your blog, you can always buy premium templates from the web.

IMPORTANT: Google recently started discouraging templates on their search engines that aren't responsive to different viewing sources. By that, I mean that most people now look at websites on their mobile phones. Consider a template that works well on all devices (these are called responsive templates) – iPads, Android tablets etc. Most themes will tell you how well they integrate with handheld devices.

You can also add free plugins via the PlugIn section. These are little bits of software that add features to your blog – things like statistics, sign-up forms etc. Askimet is usually included free with Wordpress and this attempts to block spam comments on your posts which you will encounter. It's worth signing up for this, as comments add to your storage load on your server. I've had a few sites pulled because the huge amount of spam comments has dragged it down. It's a bit like using up all your storage on your mobile phone.

Here are a few other plugins that I use. Search for them in the PlugIns>Add New button.

\-   **Wordfence.** Sadly some robots do try to take over your blog and Wordfence should stop this. It's free and is used by loads of people, including me.

\-   **SEO by Yoast**. This is a great plugin that will supercharge your posts to allow them to be picked up by search engines. I'll discuss SEO a little later.

\-   **Subscribe.** Visitors to your site can subscribe to your posts and it's worth getting a highly-rated plugin that can easily capture email addresses, which you can use to contact your audience directly.

\-   **Forms.** Adding a contact form to your blog will give it a professional touch and will allow you to hear directly from your loving audience.

\-   **Catchpa.** You will have come across these boxes when you're filling in forms online. They're the squiggly looking letters and numbers that you have to type in to prove that you are human (presuming of course, that you are). It's designed to stop spammers.

There is a huge range of plugins for almost anything that you want to do with your blog but bear in mind that the more plugins you have, the more it'll put a burden on your server. Page loading times can be affected by a large number of plugins and having too many will also detract from people reading your content, which is ultimately what you want your visitors to do. Plugins can also be susceptible to hacks from outside sources and they can bring down your blog. Wordpress will tell you when there are updates available for each of your plugins.

Spend a decent amount of time setting your blog up. Imagine that you are a visitor and try and experience it from their point of view. You can of course, change things as you go along so don't spend months.

It's the next chapter that will set your blog apart from the others. Are you finally ready to find out how I got 1 million visits in seven months? ('Hasn't he got to it yet?)

Ok. Here it is.

PART FOUR

The Importance of Good Content

I touched up on this earlier when I spoke about the magazines I set up with my business partner. Your content has to be of good quality. Content IS king, as clichéd as that sounds. As a former English teacher, I'm a former Chief Constable of the Grammar Police too. Poor quality writing shows. If you are unsure about spelling and grammar, ask a friend to look it over before you post it. Scan it with Spellchecker. To this day, even I still have to Google certain ways of doing things – how to use semicolons, how to punctuate dialogue, etc. The beauty of the internet is that it's all there for you to learn – just look for it!

Remember to paragraph your work. There's nothing worse or off-putting for a reader than trawling through a huge block of writing to find the information they want. If you're not sure how and when to paragraph your work, Google it. Self-learn. It's pretty simple. When I write my blogs for WalesOnCraic, I draft them on Word first. Word usually flags up any typos and when I've finished, I read the post out loud to myself (the dog thinks I'm reading it to him, the pleb) to see if it makes sense. The posts I publish on WalesOnCraic tend to be spoof news stories, which follow a journalistic style.

Here's how I structure my news stories:

-        Leading paragraph (I aim for one sentence maximum) that sums up the entire story.
-        The second paragraph expands on the first one, and usually adds names to the characters and locations of the story.
-        The third paragraph will be a quote from the main subject or character. This could run up to about four or five sentences at most, but no more.
-        The fourth paragraph highlights the story from another angle – maybe another character affected by the main story.
-        The final paragraph is the least important but usually rounds off the story in one way or another.

Can you see how I structure the story? I use this technique for most of my stories. It's the journalistic way of writing because it's a 'news' story. I've never been taught that by anyone – it's something I taught myself but you will come across it in any newspaper. The idea is that the leading paragraph sums up the story in one or two sentences. As the story goes on, the details in the story become less and less important. The reason for this is that journalists submit their stories to the subeditor, who cuts the story to size, depending on what room they have in the paper or magazine. Of course, with the internet, you tend not to have limited room but I still use that style to create a 'newsy' blog. Read the work of other people who write what you want to write and learn from them. Study their style and structure.

Your blog will probably be a totally different kind of blog to mine - it maybe a recipe blog; it may be a collection of short stories or poems or it may be a blog of your journey through an illness or health issue. That's fine. My structure will most likely not suit what you are doing. It's likely that you already know about structuring an article or blog post. It's your blog and you know it better than anyone.

But when it comes to creating viral content, there is one concept that will set your blog post apart from others and get you lots of visitors. It's a basic, human and very powerful notion that shapes the world that we live in. I'll tell you about it in the next chapter.

Why Do People Share Stuff On Social Media?

My best friend Danielle is a psychologist – I met her when I was 18 and have been alongside her through her A Levels all the way through to being a Highly Specialised Clinical Psychologist. Instead of going to my university to do my degree, I'd often visit her in for weeks on end at her university. While she was out at lectures, I'd have nothing else to do other than read her psychology books (this was the early 1990s when we had no internet remember). Those books taught me a lot.

Let's look at the reasons why people share content on social media:
-        They connect with what's been written and want to share it with their friends.
-        They want people to see things from their point of view.
-        They want to look cool and 'with it'. I call them sheep – they feel that they have to share something because everyone else is. Think 'Ice Bucket Challenge' and you'll get the idea.
-        They think that by sharing something, they will encounter good luck (or avoid bad luck). Annoying.
-        Someone famous has died. Don't ask me why, but people love sharing news like this. If anyone out there wants to set up a blog with all the latest celebrity

deaths on it, I'm sure it'd do very well indeed.

Let's look at this in more detail with an example of one of my viral posts.

One of my first posts on WalesOnCraic was a list of 'Places to Visit In Barry'. Barry is a small seaside town in South Wales - that's where I'm from so I know the place pretty well. I didn't publish the post willy-nilly. I posted this post knowing that my target audience (the people of Barry) would love it and CONNECT with it. It's like seeing your hometown on TV. I knew that once a person from Barry had read it, they'd want to share it with their friends from Barry so that they make another connection. I figured that if Barry has a population of 40,000 people, a good percentage of them would want to share it. And they did. I can almost hear them saying 'Ha! Look at this!' Even the local newspaper, *The Barry and District News* picked up on it – fame at last!

A month later, I posted a fictional story about a lad from Prestatyn (a North Wales town) who attended a Hallowe'en party dressed as Wolverine (a topical post as it was Hallowe'en). The story was that he tried to scratch his arse, forgetting he had blades for fingers, and chopped his todger off. So what do the people of Prestatyn do? They share it. I even had people commenting with 'it could only happen in Prestatyn' (except the only place it happened was in my head). People like to think that their perceived group are 'mad' or different in some way but ultimately, we are all the same. You need to appeal to these people who think that they are somehow different from the rest. It was one of these kind of posts that made me realise that my site was about to become a 'monster'.

Here's another example that shows a SHARED EXPERIENCE combined with a TOPICAL POST.

In February 2015, Wales played England at the Millennium Stadium (back to the rugby again I'm sorry). Of course, Wales lost and I, in my mostly drunk state, posted a short story about Wales 'deliberately losing to England to make England think that we were crap ahead of the World Cup so that they wouldn't bother training hard'. The two teams would meet again a few months later. I published the post within minutes of the game finishing and within an hour, the post had been shared over 40,000 times on Facebook. By who? Welsh people who were still hurting from the loss and wanting some kind of laugh. People like me, who were drunk and were 'trigger happy' with their Share button. The servers went into meltdown after about 90 minutes before my site went down. I earned £100 off that one post alone and had my servers held out, Lord knows how much I could have earned. If your blog starts reaching these kinds of moments, you will need to look at getting yourself a dedicated or virtual server. Speak to your host if this happens. They'll be more than happy to help you out and relieve you of a few hundred quid.

I had to upgrade my dedicated server to handle the traffic because the site was not working whenever anything went viral. I couldn't even log in! My good friend Howard said that he had never seen anything like it. The boys and girls at Pinnacle Internet Marketing, Cardiff did all the technical work of moving the website to my new server and that's where the site remains to this day. You should be able to find a good local company who can help you with this if you need it. A dedicated server will cost you but if you are drawing in those kinds of stats on a regular basis, you will seriously need to consider it. It's a good investment as you can provide a stable blog that people will be happy to use and recommend to their friends. It will

34

also serve to earn you some income. Once you've recouped your costs, the rest of pure profit.

I always remember my first ever boss telling me that you have to invest to get money back. For years, I was a tightwad and always tried to do things on the cheap. It does ultimately show - there is no such thing as a free lunch and you do get what you pay for in this world.

How To Write Viral Posts

To figure out how to get people to your blog, it's worth looking at some of the things that you look at and share yourself online. Ultimately, the stuff you look at online could be one of many things but blog posts that do well are ones that contain a very special element. Once I tell you what it is, you'll kick yourself for not realising it sooner.

It's called a SHARED experience. Think about it. Look at your own Facebook page. Why are you sharing what you share? Is it because you can identify with what you've posted? Maybe you are hoping that some of your friends or family will 'like' it because it's something you've shared together.

It all comes down to the shared experience. People share WalesOnCraic stuff because they are Welsh and can connect with what I post. They can connect with the language, the places, the dialect, the things we say and the way we say them. They want to share it with their friends because they too, have that shared experience of the Welsh way of life. You can apply that shared experience to anything that you like. Music, art, pastimes – anything that bonds you to your audience. They become part of your world and vice versa. This is why it is so critical to decide on a target audience before you start writing.

Before I dream up my next spoof news story, I

sometimes try and imagine a post that someone would share with the comment 'This is SO me'. Or if someone is going to share the post on a friend's timeline, I imagine them commenting with something like 'Is this you?' I try and envisage people's responses.

When it comes to content, and if you're looking to get people to your blog, I find that it comes down to two categories:

Universal Content – these are the type of posts that someone could discover two years later and will still be fresh. It's not time-specific. On WalesOnCraic, one of the most popular posts we ran was '10 Freakiest Towns in Wales'. Again, this post had a niche, was presented in the form of a list (always popular) and its content was genuinely funny (you can view it at www.walesoncraic. com/top-10-freakiest-welsh-villages)

Universal posts are the bread and butter of your blog – they're the glue that holds the blog together. But if you want to go REALLY viral, and to draw huge figures to your blog, you need to post topical stuff. This is the other category.

Topical Content - These are the posts that, if done correctly, could see you having to fork out for a new server. That's how explosive these posts can be! I'll give you two examples:

WalesOnCraic was launched at the back end of August 2014. At the time, our capital city Cardiff, was gearing up for a visit by the bigwigs of NATO. It was an unprecedented occasion – President Obama was the big name heading to the city.

One morning, as I was driving my wife into work in the city, we noticed a large security fence being erected up around Cardiff Castle. This was where the state dinner would take place in early September. As the days went on, the fence got longer and bigger, to the point where the city seemed as if it was under siege.

It became a real hot topic on my Facebook profile so, trying to latch onto that, I posted a post entitled '7 Things You Can Do In Cardiff While NATO Is On'. You can read it here www.walesoncraic.com/7-things-south-wales-nato-summit, but the gist of it was that for each thing on the list, you couldn't do it because NATO had taken over that particular venue. It was, in keeping with the site, a tongue in cheek post highlighting that NATO was stopping us doing what we wanted as city-goers. I published the post, making sure I had NATO in the headline and it brought in a fair amount of traffic, as people could identify with the narrative.

NATO arrived – the big occasion was the state dinner at Cardiff Castle and the big question everyone was asking was what route the Obama cavalcade was going to take into the city. With Cardiff Castle trending on social media, I had to think of something amusing that would use the words 'Cardiff' and 'Castle'. What I ended up with was a short 'news' story about a taxi driver taking Obama to Castle Bingo instead of Cardiff Castle. Again, I was looking for that connection with my niche (Welsh people LOVE playing bingo) and that post, combined with the earlier one (and a few original viral pictures) saw my Facebook page light up. I also saw a huge amount of traffic to my blog. It was all about the SHARED EXPERIENCE of my visitors – most of them had experienced the 'Ring of Steel' fence around the castle (and its frustrations of trying to get to where you wanted) and most people thought it was funny that Obama, Head of the Free World, would have gotten into a taxi AND visited our local bingo hall. They then wanted to share it with their friends. The site drew over 50,000 visits that week.

Can you see how topical posts create a perfect storm? And as well as reacting to real-world events, you can pre-empt things by looking ahead and planning posts around forthcoming events.

If You Are Looking To Sell Services Or Products Via Your Website

I speak to many advertisers and many potential advertisers in and around Cardiff for my magazines who tell me that they've got a website supporting their products and services. That's great news.

I also speak to businesses owners who pay internet companies to take care of their websites for them. They entrust these expensive internet companies (sometimes in another country), who know nothing about the business they are writing for, to drive people to their door. This isn't so good.

Here's the problem:

Creating content for your website isn't easy. But ask yourself this:

Is the content of your website actually helping you sell your services or products?

Most business owners will reflect on this and go quiet. They realise that their content is not driving people to their website and converting potential sales.

If they do decide to create some content, they'll pick a topic about their industry at random and write about it. They will then post the article to social media and maybe send out an email to their mailing list.

Ultimately though, they will then hope that people who have come across their article will, by some stroke of luck, be sufficiently interested enough in a particular (and usually non-related!) service or product. Sound familiar? I know I've done it a lot in the past, I can guarantee you that!

Here's the solution:

As I've said before, it's an old cliché, but 'Content is

king'. Adding relevant content to your website, if you have one, is a powerful way of converting potential customers to actual customers.

So if you want to produce content that supports and sells your products and services, here's how to do it. Think of the END RESULT and work backwards.

a) Begin by asking yourself which of your services or products you want to sell

b) Decide on who you think would buy this service or product

c) Break your target audience down even further into smaller categories

d) Put yourself in their shoes and think about what questions they might have about your service and product

e) Pre-empt them by answering those questions and writing this down as your content

f) Add a link to the content that will sell your service or product, or at very least, put them in touch with you

g) Add relevant and specific keywords, especially in your heading and the first line of your content to supercharge your Search Engine Optimisation

Ta-da! That's it!

Decide on what you want to sell and write your content around that specific service or product! It may take an hour or so but the reward will be more potential customers connecting with you. Don't waste time (or money) writing about things with no purpose.

Headings

Earlier in this section, I was speaking about setting your permalinks for your posts. These form the URLs (web addresses) that you share. Wordpress will automatically create a URL based on your heading so bear in mind that your heading should contain one or two keywords that relate to the post.

Let's say that you are writing a post about how to make Yorkshire puddings from scratch. Let's say that you run with a heading of 'These are delicious any time of the year'. Wordpress will allocate your URL as www.yourblognamehere.com/these-are-delicious-any-time-year. Or something similar.

Now let's say that someone is searching the web for Yorkshire Puddings. What chance do you think they have of finding your post if it has a heading like the one above? That's right. None. What you want is a heading that says 'How To Make Yorkshire Puddings from Scratch'. Wordpress will generate a URL that looks something like www.yourblognamehere.com/yorkshire-puddings-from-scratch. (If you get it wrong first time, you can edit them but try not to change it once you've shared the post, as people won't be directed to the new, revised URL).

A good way to decide on your heading is to think backwards. What keywords would you type into Google if you were looking for something specific? Use the keywords that you would use in your headings. Keep your headings as short as possible too with just enough information in them to entice people to the post.

SEO (Search Engine Optimisation)

Search Engine Optimisation is a massive thing when it comes to attracting 'organic' traffic. By this, I mean people coming across your blog via search engines, as opposed to reacting to something you've shared on social media.

One important thing you need to know: Google doesn't rank entire websites in terms of relevance. It ranks individual pages or posts.

If you're using Wordpress like I do, there is a great free plugin that will help you with this (it's the SEO by Yoast one I mentioned a little while ago). It'll add sections to your post on your dashboard before posting that will give your post a good SEO rating. There are a few things you should do to improve your SEO:

- Think of your target audience and decide on your keywords. These are the words that you think your audience will be looking for.
- Make your content more than 300 words (mine tend to be shorter than that on WalesOnCraic because my stories are slightly unusual).
- Include your keyword in the headline AND the first line of your text.
- Don't overuse your keywords. Google is clever enough to know what you're trying to do and dismiss your page if it's flooded with the same keywords.
- Add an image. Make sure that you save your image on to your computer using your keyword in the title as opposed to just 'Image 1'. Someone searching Google is more likely to pick up an image that is relevant that way. Again, try and narrow it to your niche. I'll give you an example:

A few years ago I interviewed the world's most expensive footballer Gareth Bale for the local magazines that I publish. Search Gareth Bale on Google and you'll find millions of references. To get myself onto the first page of Google (at time of writing, although my interview has been sat there for a few years) I decided to include the keywords 'Gareth Bale' and 'Whitchurch' (my local village) in the same Heading. Type in 'Gareth Bale Whitchurch' into Google and see if it's still there. Even if it's on page 2 or 3 of the Google listings, it's still not bad considering all the other millions of references to him. This is what I mean by narrowing your niche. Someone searching Gareth Bale and Whitchurch is the type of person I want to attract to my site anyway so it's a winner for me. If I was to set up a blog about how to get into drag racing, I'd use keywords such as 'take part' and 'drag racing' in my headlines and on my images.

So, in short, create a post that is relevant to your chosen target audience and craft your blog in a way that will make it easy for your target audience to find you. Even if the post does go viral after sharing it on social media (I'm about to show you how you can do that), it's always good practice to have good SEO on every post.

Right. Now that you've got a potential viral post ready to go, you're going to have to start sharing it on social media. Here's how:

Using Social Media To Drive Traffic To Your Blog

I've read a lot of stuff about the power of Twitter but to be honest, it was Facebook that drove over 1 million visits to my blog in seven months. For me, Facebook allows me to provide more blurb about the story when I post to it. It could be a quote from the post, allowing people to see the style it's written in. It could also be a call to action.

At the time of writing, my WalesOnCraic Facebook page only has 12k followers. I say 'only' but I say this in context with a lot of niche competitors' sites that have a lot more. Fortunately for me, that's where they stop! Imagine having instant access to over 50k people but not being able to sell them anything!

My Facebook page is made up of the following:

- Posts from my website.
- Viral pictures (or memes) created by me.
- Viral pictures (or memes) created by others, but shared on the page as I think my target audience might appreciate them (and hopefully share them).

So what's the big deal about sharing stuff?

Well, this is it: **A SHARE IS FREE ADVERTISING**. Read that again and think about it properly. **A SHARE IS FREE ADVERTISING**. Businesses pay big money to have their web addresses seen by other people. You see them on billboards, the sides of taxis. People pay money to have their websites put on TV, on radio, on the internet itself and even on bald men's heads. But here's the thing – you don't have to fork out any money for it. Add your web address to everything you do – even if it doesn't go viral straight away, it could do a few months down the line. As well as creating a brand that people will come to recognise, you are advertising your website for free. And when people share it, they are doing the hard work for you.

This applies to pictures and images too. Your followers will share the picture with their friends, thinking that they're sharing a picture. Technically, they are, but guess what? They're also sharing your website address with all their friends! It's FREE advertising! If people like the content of the picture (and who have never come across your site), and if it strikes a chord with them (that SHARED EXPERIENCE I was talking about), it's possible that they might want to click on your website to see where the picture originated from. They may want to be part of your club. I know it's something I've done in the past. Think of things from the viewer's point of view.

Here's what you need to do if you want to create a Facebook viral explosion:

-      Set up a Facebook Page if you haven't done this already.

I won't go into too much into detail about setting up a Facebook page, as it's all fairly self-explanatory but make sure that you have a good Cover Photo and Profile Picture. (check dimensions and crop as necessary). You will also want to add your website address and details of what your site is about. Your Facebook page is going to be one of the main ways that people arrive at your site so it needs to look as professional as you can.

-      Write a Post That Has Viral Potential (see previous chapter)

-      Post your Blog Posts to Facebook

Ok, that all sounds pretty straightforward but hopefully, if you've put the groundwork in as I've described previously, you should see 'likes' and 'shares' popping up. There are a few things to bear in mind though.

It's taken me a while master the art of posting blogs on Facebook – namely because Facebook can be pretty temperamental when it comes to posting them. When you post a link to Facebook, it's a lot more powerful with a picture linked to it. You may have come across this when you post a link to your Facebook and there is no picture. Looks crap doesn't it? No one is going to click on a link. Some people are more visual than others.

So. Here's how I do it:

Copy the address URL of the post you want to share (i.e. your blog post) using right-click and 'Copy'.
Go to your Facebook page. Paste the URL into the Status Box and wait for Facebook to populate it with a picture. If you have correctly set a 'Featured Picture' on your post via your Wordpress dashboard, the link should populate with this picture. If it doesn't happen,

you may want to refresh/reload your Facebook page and try again. Most of the time, this should now populate your link with the picture. If it still doesn't add one, you may want to manually 'add' a picture although I think that this lessens the impact of the URL, which is ideally what you want your reader to click on.

If you still have no picture appearing, or if you have some other picture that's not relevant, you can try using the Facebook Debugger. Google it, insert the copied URL of your post and click 'Fetch New Scrape'. Sounds a bit grim but you should end up with the picture that you were after.

If you're technically minded, you may want to research a bit more into how Facebook works. I'm not a tech-geek so have figured out ways around some of Facebook's quirks, which do change from time to time.

Before You Click 'Post'

Once you are inside your Facebook Status Box and have inserted your URL, click the cursor BEFORE the link and type in something that is going to make your reader want to click on the link. Popular examples are 'I can't believe this' or 'Would you do this?' If you want a more 'sedate' headline, try and copy what others do. WalesOnline.com are good at this – they may take a short snippet from the story that entices the reader and makes them want to click on it. Ask the question that the reader will want to know the answer to by reading the post.

Click 'Post' when you are happy that the spelling is correct and that it makes sense. I like to give my URL link its own line to sit on. You can tag people in your post if you like, but I prefer not to do this, as I don't like to involve people without their permission.

Share the link on Twitter at the same time, remembering to add hash tags for keywords that you think will help drive people to your post. If you have any other social media accounts, do this now.

On no account, ask your reader to 'Share This' on every post. They are not your employees and they'll soon get pissed off. The aim is to create a post that people WANT to share off their own back.

Don't go sharing other people's viral stuff straight from their page either. If you find something that's relevant to your target audience, and you think that they'd appreciate it, right-click on your mouse and save the picture to your computer and upload it to your page. THEN share it – that way, if it's 'doing the rounds' on the net, when it gets shared from your page, they'll be sharing YOUR picture and not someone else's.

One note on copyright here. The internet is a murky place and it's likely that you will want to use images to feature in your post. I received a phone call just a week ago from a guy with a gripe about some work I'd published. I'd put one of his photos in my magazine (which had been submitted to me in good faith from a local camera club) but this guy wasn't happy. Not at all. It seems the camera club forwarded it to me without his permission. I wasn't to blame, but I went around his house to apologise all the same. He was local and we've since become good friends. But the internet is a big place and most people won't be as forgiving. Be wary.

A quick word about competitors pages too – a similar kind of page to mine called *The Welsh Bible* got itself 50,000 Facebook 'likes' in less than two months, simply by posting videos and pictures (some stolen directly from us). Of course, 50k seems better than 12k but I'd prefer to have 12k genuine followers than 50k who like it thanks to one viral video. Don't get too carried away focusing about how many people 'like' your

Facebook page or how many Twitter followers you have. Remember that you're catering for your dedicated target audience. Ideally, you want to get people OFF Facebook and onto your blog so take time to appreciate the people who do visit.

IMPORTANT: Facebook can be a bit of a psycho. By that, I mean that it can be a bit temperamental. Back in 2010, I ran a Facebook account for Derek the Weathersheep which attracted 5,000 Facebook friends (their limit at the time) within a few months. Facebook then cottoned on that my profile was set up as a personal account when in fact, it should have been set up as a page. In their great wisdom, they closed my account down, saying that my name wasn't a real name. They asked me to send a copy of my passport to prove that my real name was Derek the Weathersheep (I couldn't) and despite many emails to them, they never responded. In an instant, my 5,000 followers were wiped out. Facebook is also a bit of a prude when it comes to nudity too. They're happy to allow violent videos and pictures but for some reason, they don't like bare flesh. Be responsible in what you post – it could come back to bite you on the arse later.

Twitter

Up until now, my Twitter account has been nowhere near as productive as my Facebook account. For me, Twitter has been my 'reserve' outlet that I tweet links to my blog from. It did bring in a lot of traffic when I first set up (more on that shortly) but my current stats don't indicate that it currently brings in much.

Having said that, there is of course, HUGE potential for Twitter that I have overlooked – I admit that! In prepping this book for launch, I've come across like-minded publishers and bloggers who have tens of thousands of followers. A few of those retweeting your post would see your stats go through the roof! And I'm only just finding that out!

While you're reading this, I'm currently rolling up my sleeves and getting stuck into Twitter. One thing I have learned is that if you're looking to promote anything on Twitter, there's one big thing that you need to do – and that's put yourself into the position of other people. Ask yourself this question: 'would you follow you if you were someone else?'

If you have a Twitter account, you may have come across people who are constantly trying to promote their blog or new book. They go on and on and on about it. The more they tell you to look at it, the more likely you are to click 'Unfollow' and never see them again. I've just finished reading a great book called *How To Gain 100,000 Followers On Twitter* by M LeMont (which you can find on Amazon). I'm not going to reveal their secrets here (that would be grossly unsporting of me) but it has hit home that there are few things that you do need to be doing to create a good Twitter base. Building good relationships and helping to promote other people's work is critical. In short, the more you engage with people, the more successful and respected you will be. Retweet other people's stuff more than your own. People will then flock to you and your expertise and hopefully follow you looking for a retweet themselves.

Your blog may work better on Twitter – find out what works for you. I'm still finding my feet right now and it's highly likely that you're better at it than I am. Just remember to be polite to those who you come across – they could help you later on down the line. Find me at @patric__morgan and say hi.

Viral Images

I've spent many years teaching myself how to use
Photoshop and similar software that now allow me to
create images. For WalesOnCraic, as it's a humorous
site, I'll usually find a funny image from the web and
add some wording that's in keeping with the site. I
apply the same technique as I do for web content – I
rely heavily on the shared experience I keep banging on
about, and I use the same dialect and language as my
target audience. Keep in mind your target audience. I'll
give you an example. Here in Wales, one of the more
famous gateways to our country from England is the
Severn Bridge. As you head into Wales, there's a sign
that reads 'Croeso y Gymru', which means 'Welcome
to Wales'. I've passed it hundreds of times, and judging
by the queues at the toll booths, so have many tens of
thousands.

I found a picture of the sign, put it in Photoshop and
added the words 'The only road sign in Wales that will
make you smile'. I added my website address to the
picture and shared it on social media.

Naturally, it struck a chord with those tens of
thousands who have passed the sign. The picture
went viral, and because it had my website address on
it (and alongside the post so that it became a live link
that people could click on), it both helped with my
branding, my Facebook 'likes', plus I saw a spike of
people visiting my blog.

So create viral images, in keeping with your blog, to
attract new visitors and to help promote your blog.

Listly

(NB: This is not a social media site) I mention Listly
here although it should technically appear in the

previous chapter about content. But the reason I put it here is its sharing potential. People love lists and 'Top 10s', especially if they contain images. Buzzfeed has led the way on this over the years and Listly is a similar tool. Head over to www.list.ly and sign up for an account. I created a few lists with Listly when I first set up my blog. What I wasn't expecting was Listly's CEO, Nick Kellet to be able to see our content (no idea why this never occurred to me). He loved the content and kept sharing them with his thousands of followers, ironically on Twitter. It was also his way of showing the power of lists (and his software) and he'd then share our content and show how effective lists were. It was a win-win situation. He was showcasing our lists and we were showcasing his software.

Get Subscribers To Your Blog

A good way to add visitor numbers to your blog is to add a Subscribe form to your blog. An email address is a valuable commodity, since you can contact your followers directly should you lose your blog for some reason. I use Mailchimp to collect email addresses. It's pretty handy at collating addresses and you can also send out bulk emails if for instance, you've got a new blog post out etc. Depending on your (and their) settings, subscribers will be sent an email every time you post a new post – the more subscribers, the more they will click on your posts. Simples!

Building a mailing list is also important if you are looking to make money from your blog. If you decide to add merchandise to your blog, it's easy to bang out a mailshot announcing your new range.

PART FIVE

Monetising your site

You may remember my blog called Derek the Weathersheep. I think I've mentioned it enough.

Good. Well here's a little ditty that made me realise that I could make money from my blog.

One grumbly rainy day, when I was working on this blog, I came across an audio recording of Jordan (one of the UK's less talented celebrities) singing without autocue. As you can imagine, it was pretty horrific. Imagine the sound of a drowning cat combined with the sound of sharp nails screeching slowly down a blackboard. It was that bad.

I posted the YouTube link on my site and then shared it on Facebook. It got a few likes, nothing spectacular. A short while later, I went shopping with my wife and when I got home, I clicked on my site, only to find that the site had gone down. I got on the blower to my hosts, who told me that the site had received too much traffic and that it was bringing down all their other sites that were sharing the same server. Cut a long story short, one of my followers had posted the link to Jordan's Facebook page, which had well over 3 million fans. Of course, 3 million Jordan fans wanted to see what their hero sounded like without autotune. Talk about target market! I got the site back up but I had to take the post down – it was crippling my site plus it wasn't my content in any case.

A few hours later, I checked my Adsense account out

of curiosity and found that the one post had drawn in £40. Ok, that doesn't sound like much but seeing as I'd only ever got pennies up until then, it was something mega for me. I felt like I had struck gold. It was then that I realised that I could make money off the blog, as long as I was clever about it. I can't remember the name of the lad who posted it to Jordan's Facebook, but whoever you are, I owe you a pint or two!

Banner Advertising

If you are drawing big numbers, you can start charging businesses for Banner Adverts. These are adverts that you can add manually to different parts of your site, usually with a link through to the business that bought the advert off you. I'll be honest - I've never fully explored this side of making money but I know from reading about others than you can add it to your revenue streams if you put the work in.

Adsense

I make a fair bit of money through Google Adsense. With this, you receive a small amount of revenue every time someone clicks on one of the adverts that appear on your site.

You'll need to set up an Adsense account and once you've done that, you can create different types of adverts. It's then a case of copying the code and manually inserting it into the dedicated sections (or if you are confident enough with HTML) in your posts. There are also plugins for your Wordpress that will analyse your pages and insert adverts for you if you'd rather do things that way. Don't over populate your posts with adverts (Google only allows three per page anyway) or try and click your own adverts to increase revenue because, as I said earlier, Google is clever. It'll know, and ban you from having an account.

Spend time figuring out what works and what doesn't. I tend to have one Adsense banner advert running underneath my post heading and before the main text. It's quite possible that someone wanting to scroll down to read the post could click on it – I still get paid for it!

Content Click

You will have come across some websites where, instead of adverts, you get given links that offer to take you to other sites. These are often paid links and works in a similar way to Adsense in that if someone clicks on the link, you get a small commission.

Content Click is great programme that I've signed up for. The best thing about it is that they pay about FIVE times more than Adsense do. You do need to sign up as a publisher (at www.contentclick.co.uk) and they will look at your site and make a decision so this is worth looking at once your stats are starting to look good.

Merchandise

Depending on the type of blog you're running, you may want to offer some merchandise to your followers. This is particularly useful if you're running a blog for a charity or if you have a strong brand. Here are some good ways that I top up my income. Fabrily (www. fabrily.com) is a site where you can make some quick money printing T-shirts by running 'campaigns' which can run for a few days or up to a week. The site is designed primarily for charities to raise money so if your blog is running along these lines, it's well worth a look. I used the site to make some profit for myself although the idea soon dried up when I milked it too hard. I now use Dizzyjam.com (www.dizzyjam.com) to provide a permanent online 'shop' for my merchandise. As well as T-shirts, you can add mugs, bags etc. The site is designed for band merchandise but I've tweaked my account for my own purposes. There are plenty of other sites that offer similar services – do your research and find out what's best for you.

TIP: Uploading artwork to sites such as these usually work best with PNG files. A PNG is similar to a JPEG, but with a PNG, you can remove any annoying backgrounds (or make them transparent) from your picture. There is an excellent piece of free software that allows you to do this called Paint.net. Make sure you get it from www.getpaint.net/index.html where it is available to download for free.

To create a PNG file, upload the JPEG that you want the background removed from, then use the magic wand tool to highlight the bit you want to remove (you can play around with the Tolerance setting in the top bar to highlight any background you want to remove). Click EDIT>CUT to remove what you've highlighted. Then save it as a PNG, not a JPEG. This will save your picture without the annoying background and gives it a more professional look when it's printed out on T-shirts and other merchandise.

Books

I'm a writer by trade so it was only natural that I'd want to make books. I planned my first WalesOnCraic book so that the second book would be ready in November – perfect as that Christmas gift. Having the first book already published also gave me the option of doubling my money. I have several other books which I have published off the back of my blogs, notably my *Fifteen Grades of Hay* trilogy from Derek the Weathersheep. I had originally designed the cover as a spoof cover to get a laugh on Facebook but after it got so many likes on Facebook, I decided to actually write it. The three books aren't very long, and priced for 'impulse buys' but they've sold in their thousands. I wrote the second and third instalments while my father was dying. It might sound a bit odd that I was writing something so 'out-there' at such a critical time in my life but it was one way that I could escape from the horror of what was happening before my eyes.

Throughout the process of my Dad's cancer, I did keep an online journal of the everyday accounts on Blogger as a way of coping. I wasn't intending for anyone to read it – I simply wanted to get things down. However, I soon started getting comments saying that my dad would be proud and, giving in to my ego, I posted it on Facebook to share with my friends. Despite its futile tone, its content struck a chord with many people, especially on Twitter. As I finished the blog, I noticed that WalesOnline, our national news site, were running a national blogging competition. I hesitated before nominating myself, thinking that it was all rather vain, but in the end, I did it for Dad. I was shortlisted and attended the awards ceremony at Welsh College of Music and Drama and much to my surprise, found that I won. I had some kind of speech rehearsed in my head, just in case I won but as I left my seat, my wife told me to keep it short. By the time I got to my microphone, I was caught in two minds and ultimately talked a load of bollocks. I cringe every time I think about it. But I had an award under my belt. That was important because I could now sell myself as an 'award-winning' writer – something to set me apart from other writers.

The book is available at my site www.patricmorgan.

co.uk. All proceeds go to Velindre Cancer Hospital. It's a bit of a tearjerker but if you want to see what kind of writing wins awards, it's worth a look.

In the same vein, I have a good friend who set up a blog relating to her diagnosis of MS. She recently turned her blog into a book in the same way that I did and is receiving rave reviews on Amazon. Again, it's that targeted audience that makes the statistics needle move.

You can publish your book on Amazon at Createspace.com. This allows you to also publish it for Kindle. There are some excellent resources of publishing your own books online and that's where I learnt how to do it all.

I have also published a Christmas book for Derek the Weathersheep – it sells well at Christmas (obviously) and is designed as a stocking filler for followers of Derek.

PART SIX

Maintaining Momentum and Evolving

Keeping things going needs motivation. As I sit here writing this, I'm sat overlooking the huge volcanic caldera in Santorini. I've had my breakfast and this is the first time I've written for about three weeks. I've been working so hard that I've burned myself out. Only now is that fire coming back to me. Like I said in the planning stage, this is why you need to have a passion for your blog – something that comes naturally to you after you've recovered.

I remember interviewing John Dawes, the famous Welsh rugby legend who coached the only ever British and Irish Lions to a series win over the All Blacks. We were sat in his local pub one winter's afternoon and the one thing that stuck in my mind was him putting his pint down and telling me that you always have to learn from the opposition. If you have a unique blog, you will one day, find that someone somewhere has set up something similar. I embrace competition because it keeps me on my toes and stops making me lazy. After the interview, I sat with Barry John and Mervyn Davies (who sadly died a few months later). They were lovely, normal people, but inside, they all had that trait – be the best that you can at what you do. If you can apply a little of that attribute to your own blog, you'll go a long way. Don't judge your blog to other people's blogs either – judge yourself by what your targets are.

I for one am terrible at starting things and never

finishing them. Not sure if it's a 'man thing' but I've bought several blog domains and yet to even install them! This is why I said at the beginning, do something that you are passionate about – something that is part of you.

Your Fanbase

A deep fanbase is better than a wide one. Remember that you want to appeal directly to your fanbase, whether it is 10, 100 or 10,000. Serve it to them and they will do the rest because they will want to spread the message that they feel connected to. I'm a vegetarian and I've always had the idea that I'd set up a vegetarian blog one day. Vegetarianism would be my niche (although I could probably narrow that down even further for more impact – maybe how crap restaurants are at doing veggie food!). Find yourself 100 relevant followers on social media – post a blog, they'll share it with their friends because they want their friends to see it and connect with them.

PART SEVEN

Onward and Upward

I'm hoping that you've found parts of this book useful. As I mentioned at the beginning, I wanted to share my story to help you get the most out of your blog. Even if you've picked out one or two tricks, it should go some way to helping you improve your visitors' stats.

One word of caution - don't go expecting fantastic results overnight. It can happen but for the most part (and as was the case for a few of my other blogs), it'll be a slow-burning process, with peaks and troughs along the way. I was only reading this morning that the creators of Angry Birds had designed 53 games and were almost broke when they struck on the Angry Bird idea – and look what happened to them! My guess is that those 53 games, although not big hitters, were their learning curve. That's where they learned and honed their craft.

WalesOnCraic was a similar kind of story – most of it came about through making mistakes on other blogs and learning from them. It's called experience, and the more you work at it, the more experienced you will become. The more experienced you are, the better your work will be. The better you are, the more successful you will be. It's like a snowball. If you do start making an income, make sure you declare this to the relevant tax authorities.

I'll leave you with one thought – success for many doesn't live in their cleverness or luck. It comes down to their tenacity, their ability to keep on going and going. You can do it and hopefully, with some of the tricks I've shown you today, you'll get a little bit of help along the way.

Feel free to contact me at hello@patricmorgan.co.uk. I will respond to each and every email but sadly, as much as I'd love to help you personally, I won't be able to answer specific questions about blogging – I simply don't have the time as blogging is not my main job.

As I have said earlier, all the answers are out there on Google. And that's not just me being lazy – the best way to learn is to fail first and experience figuring out a way around it yourself. As a clever Chinese person once said: 'Tell me and I'll forget; show me and I may remember; involve me and I'll understand.'

I wish you all the very best for your blog.

As we say in Wales, 'Pob lwc!'

***

Ps. I'd be so grateful if you could leave a review about this book on Amazon. If it's a good review, thank you. If it's not so good, thank you also – I can only improve for my next book.

ABOUT THE AUTHOR

Patric Morgan is a multi-award-winning writer and publisher from Barry, Wales.

His work has featured in *The Guardian, BBC Radio Wales, The Huffington Post, Wales on Sunday, South Wales Echo, Western Mail, WM magazine, RedHanded* magazine and many other publications.

In 2012, Patric scooped 'Best Writing on a Blog' Award at the 2012 Wales Blog Awards for his blog, Do Not Go Gently, which was published 2013.

He is co-founder and co-editor of *Living Magazines Cardiff*, which picked up two major awards at the UK Independent Magazine Publisher Awards in 2014. As part of his work, Patric has interviewed stars such as Gareth Bale, Sam Warburton, 80s musician Howard Jones, Stan Stennett, Andy Fairweather-Low, Dame Tanni Grey-Thompson, Cerys Matthews, Gerald Davies, John Dawes, Howard Norris, Mervyn Davies, Matthew Pritchard and Hollywood's Alicia Witt and Vicki Abelson.

In 2014, with Anthony Bunko, he created WalesOnCraic and is its current editor and lead writer. Patric is currently working on his debut novel.

More at www.patricmorgan.co.uk

Printed in Great Britain
by Amazon